FABIAN HILL

ChatGPT for Professionals

Elevate Your Career and Enhance
Productivity with AI-Driven Solutions
(2024 Guide)

Copyright © 2024 by Fabian Hill

All rights reserved. No part of this publication may be reproduced, stored or transmitted in any form or by any means, electronic, mechanical, photocopying, recording, scanning, or otherwise without written permission from the publisher. It is illegal to copy this book, post it to a website, or distribute it by any other means without permission.

First edition

This book was professionally typeset on Reedsy.
Find out more at reedsy.com

Contents

1. Introduction to ChatGPT for Professionals — 1
2. Efficiency and Automation with ChatGPT — 4
3. Time Management with ChatGPT — 6
4. Organizing Information with ChatGPT — 9
5. Communication and Collaboration — 11
6. Professional Learning and Development — 14
7. Work-Life Balance with ChatGPT — 18
8. ChatGPT for Remote Work — 20
9. Ethical Considerations in AI-Assisted Work — 24
10. Looking Ahead: ChatGPT and the Future of Work — 28

1

Introduction to ChatGPT for Professionals

ChatGPT, developed by OpenAI, is an advanced language model capable of processing and producing text that resembles human speech. It operates on the GPT-3.5 framework and has been trained extensively on a vast array of internet text. ChatGPT comprehends natural language and generates responses that are contextually fitting and grammatically accurate. This technology holds promise for various applications such as market analysis, content generation, and customer interaction.

Professionals across different domains can leverage ChatGPT to boost their productivity and streamline their workflows. In this regard, ChatGPT serves as a tool for automating routine tasks, sparking novel ideas, and offering expert insights. For instance, enterprises can utilize ChatGPT to analyze market trends, conceive fresh product concepts, and craft persuasive marketing materials. Researchers may employ ChatGPT to aid in literature surveys, hypothesis formulation and validation, and data examination. Similarly, educators can harness ChatGPT to tailor learning experiences for students and enhance communication with parents.

Nonetheless, the utilization of AI tools like ChatGPT poses ethical dilemmas and necessitates responsible usage. Professionals must grapple with issues such as bias mitigation, privacy protection, and ensuring accountability when integrating AI into their operations. As AI technology evolves, it becomes imperative for professionals to stay abreast of current trends and adhere to best practices to ensure the effective and responsible deployment of these tools.

Understanding ChatGPT

ChatGPT, created by OpenAI, is an AI language model designed to produce text that mimics human speech when given natural language prompts. Utilizing deep learning methods, ChatGPT undergoes pre-training on extensive text data, enabling it to generate responses of high quality across diverse prompts. Its applications span natural language processing, content creation, language translation, and conversational interfaces. Functioning as a language model, ChatGPT comprehends the significance and context of natural language, thereby generating responses that are logical and pertinent to the provided prompt.

The Influence of Artificial Intelligence on Workplace Efficiency

Artificial intelligence (AI) has the potential to significantly boost productivity in professional settings. Through automating repetitive tasks, analyzing data, and offering valuable insights and suggestions, AI tools such as ChatGPT can aid professionals in working more efficiently and making more informed choices. Moreover, AI can improve teamwork and communication by facilitating seamless collaboration among team members, irrespective of their physical locations. Furthermore, AI can play a crucial role in tackling intricate problem-solving scenarios and making decisions, thereby empowering professionals to overcome complex challenges and seize emerging opportunities. In summary, AI stands poised to revolutionize professionals' work methodologies and assist them in achieving superior outcomes.

2

Efficiency and Automation with ChatGPT

ChatGPT offers the opportunity to enhance professional productivity through streamlined and automated solutions for diverse tasks. By automating mundane and repetitive tasks, it enables professionals to dedicate their attention to more intricate and valuable endeavors. Furthermore, ChatGPT aids in optimizing workflows by proposing enhancements to processes and pinpointing areas of inefficiency. It also facilitates quicker access to information, thereby expediting research and decision-making processes. Ultimately, ChatGPT empowers professionals to accomplish more within shorter timeframes and with reduced exertion, fostering heightened productivity and effectiveness in their roles.

Automating Routine Tasks

Streamlining repetitive tasks through automation offers numerous benefits such as time-saving, error reduction, and heightened efficiency within a work setting. Utilizing ChatGPT for this purpose involves training it to identify patterns and execute predetermined actions in response to specific inputs. For instance, ChatGPT can be programmed to automate tasks like sorting emails, entering data, arranging appointments, among others. This automation liberates valuable time, allowing individuals to concentrate on more critical tasks necessitating human attention. Furthermore, automating processes enhances precision and diminishes errors, ultimately enhancing productivity levels and job contentment.

Enhancing Efficiency with Artificial Intelligence

Enhancing efficiency in work processes through AI entails automating repetitive and time-consuming duties to enhance effectiveness and productivity. AI-driven solutions like ChatGPT can aid professionals by executing tasks such as arranging appointments, handling emails, creating reports, and condensing documents. By saving time and resources, professionals can concentrate on more significant tasks, resulting in heightened productivity and improved decision-making. Furthermore, AI can pinpoint inefficiencies and propose enhancements, fostering ongoing process refinement.

3

Time Management with ChatGPT

Efficiently managing time is crucial for productivity, and ChatGPT offers valuable assistance in this regard. Leveraging its natural language processing skills, ChatGPT aids professionals in automating repetitive tasks, organizing their workload, and arranging appointments and meetings. Moreover, it furnishes recommendations tailored to enhance workflow and boost productivity, aligning with individual objectives and work habits. By incorporating ChatGPT into their time management strategies, professionals can allocate more time to creative and strategic endeavors, ultimately fostering heightened productivity and achieving success.

Utilizing AI Assistance to Prioritize Tasks

Professionals can rely on ChatGPT to streamline their task prioritization process. By examining their task lists, ChatGPT offers guidance considering factors like urgency, significance, and deadlines. Moreover, it suggests an optimal task schedule, considering both task duration and the professional's available time slots.

Furthermore, ChatGPT aids in time management by issuing reminders and alerts for imminent deadlines and meetings. It also takes charge of scheduling recurring tasks such as routine reports or meetings.

Through the automation of these mundane tasks, professionals can redirect their focus towards more valuable endeavors that demand their expertise and creativity. This enhancement ultimately enhances their productivity and performance levels.

Organizing and Managing Your Schedule and Calendar

Managing schedules and calendars is crucial for professional efficiency, and ChatGPT offers valuable support in this domain. Here are various ways in which ChatGPT can aid in scheduling and calendar management:

1. Arranging meetings: ChatGPT can facilitate meeting scheduling by examining calendars to find mutually convenient times. It can also send out meeting invitations and reminders to participants.
2. Time allocation: ChatGPT can assist users in planning their day by creating schedules and allocating time slots for specific tasks. This helps ensure that important activities are completed efficiently.
3. Calendar upkeep: ChatGPT can manage calendars by adding and updating events, setting reminders, and issuing notifications.
4. Appointment rescheduling: ChatGPT can aid users in rearranging appointments by reviewing calendars and identifying alternative available slots.
5. Time zone adjustments: ChatGPT can help with time zone conversions, particularly when scheduling meetings or events involving participants from different time zones.
6. Personalized scheduling preferences: ChatGPT can adapt to users'

preferences over time, using this data to propose scheduling options that align with their work habits and preferences.

In summary, ChatGPT streamlines scheduling and calendar management tasks by automating routine activities, delivering reminders, and suggesting scheduling alternatives tailored to users' preferences and work methods. This enhances productivity and saves time in professional endeavors.

4

Organizing Information with ChatGPT

Utilizing ChatGPT within professional settings proves beneficial for structuring data effectively. Its functionality extends to sorting and tagging various materials like documents and files, streamlining the process of locating specific items. Moreover, it aids in condensing lengthy texts into summaries or abstracts, thus enabling professionals to expedite information review.

Furthermore, ChatGPT serves as a valuable tool for professionals to remain updated on industry developments. Through monitoring social media, news platforms, and other relevant sources, it sifts through information, delivering pertinent updates and alerts as they emerge.

In essence, ChatGPT enhances professionals' organization and awareness, empowering them to dedicate their attention to core tasks and enhance productivity.

Utilizing artificial intelligence for the organization and retrieval of data

Employing artificial intelligence (AI) for the organization and retrieval of data proves highly advantageous. ChatGPT, for instance, possesses the capability to automatically classify data according to its contents, streamlining the process of searching and retrieving information later on. This implementation not only conserves time but also enhances productivity across various sectors, such as healthcare, finance, and legal services.

Furthermore, ChatGPT can facilitate the development of tailored knowledge management systems, aiding professionals in the efficient storage and retrieval of information. These systems can automate tasks like data input, information retrieval, and knowledge dissemination, thereby allowing professionals to concentrate on more intricate responsibilities.

In summary, leveraging ChatGPT for data organization and retrieval enables professionals to save time, mitigate errors, and enhance the precision and uniformity of their work.

Capturing notes and summarizing meetings using ChatGPT

ChatGPT can support with note-taking and condensing meeting discussions. In real-time, it transcribes meetings and transforms them into written records. It can pinpoint the main topics covered and create concise summaries for easy future reference. This feature is beneficial for professionals who require efficient review of meeting notes later on. Furthermore, ChatGPT aids in producing meeting minutes and action points, facilitating review and follow-up by participants.

5

Communication and Collaboration

Effective communication and teamwork are crucial components of efficiency in any professional setting. ChatGPT offers a valuable solution for enhancing both.

One way ChatGPT proves beneficial is by summarizing meetings or discussions. This feature is particularly helpful for busy professionals who lack the time to go through entire recordings or lengthy transcripts. With ChatGPT, they can swiftly obtain summaries that encapsulate the main points of the conversation.

Moreover, ChatGPT aids in communication by providing prompt responses to common inquiries or issues. For instance, a human resources department might utilize ChatGPT to generate answers to frequently asked employee questions regarding benefits, policies, or procedures. This not only alleviates the workload on HR personnel but also ensures employees receive necessary information.

Another advantage of ChatGPT is its ability to foster knowledge exchange among team members. By generating summaries or insights from extensive data or research, ChatGPT enables sharing vital information with colleagues. This promotes uniform access to information within the team, facilitating informed decision-making.

Lastly, ChatGPT facilitates communication and collaboration among remote teams. Through real-time communication, information sharing, and project collaboration, team members can effectively work together regardless of their physical locations. This feature contributes to enhanced productivity and alignment towards common objectives for the entire team.

Improving Team Communication Using ChatGPT

Utilizing ChatGPT offers a multitude of avenues for enhancing team communication. One such application is its ability to facilitate real-time translation among team members conversing in different languages. Moreover, it can transcribe audio or video recordings of meetings, converting them into text for easy sharing and review. Integrating ChatGPT with platforms like Slack or Microsoft Teams enables the creation of chatbots, providing prompt responses to common inquiries or updates on ongoing projects, thereby streamlining workflow and boosting productivity.

Furthermore, ChatGPT's capability extends to generating succinct summaries of lengthy emails, reports, or articles, enabling efficient dissemination of key information within the team. This feature saves time and ensures everyone remains well-informed without the need to delve into the entire document. Lastly, ChatGPT can analyze the tone and sentiment of team communications, such as emails or chat messages, to detect potential conflicts or areas of misunderstanding. By proactively identifying such issues, team members can collaborate effectively to prevent or resolve conflicts, fostering a harmonious working environment.

Employing artificial intelligence for cooperative endeavors and idea generation.

Leveraging AI like ChatGPT can significantly enhance collaborative efforts and brainstorming sessions. One effective method is to have team members input their ideas or queries, with ChatGPT then generating responses or suggesting additional concepts. This process proves beneficial for sparking innovation, tackling challenges, and exploring diverse project approaches.

Moreover, ChatGPT serves as a valuable asset in moderating discussions and fostering debates. Team members can present questions or topics to ChatGPT, which generates responses to kickstart further discourse. This approach fosters constructive dialogue and ensures inclusivity, allowing all team members to contribute to the conversation.

In summary, ChatGPT stands as a valuable ally in promoting teamwork and communication, facilitating the generation of fresh ideas and innovative project strategies.

6

Professional Learning and Development

Professional development encompasses the ongoing enhancement of an individual's expertise, capabilities, and proficiencies pertinent to their career or vocation. ChatGPT serves as a beneficial resource to assist professionals in their educational journey. Below are various ways in which ChatGPT can contribute to professional growth:

1. Research: ChatGPT aids professionals in conducting research by aiding in tasks such as reviewing literature, formulating hypotheses, and analyzing data.
2. Knowledge acquisition: ChatGPT furnishes professionals with insights across a broad spectrum of subjects, facilitating the acquisition of new concepts and terminology within their domain.
3. Problem-solving: ChatGPT offers assistance to professionals in resolving intricate issues by furnishing suggestions and recommendations grounded in data and research.
4. Skill enhancement: ChatGPT supports professionals in honing new skills through tailored learning experiences and resource recommendations.
5. Training and education: ChatGPT serves as a tool for educational purposes, offering professionals interactive learning opportunities and

personalized feedback.
6. Networking and collaboration: ChatGPT connects professionals with peers in their field, fostering collaboration, knowledge exchange, and peer-to-peer learning.
7. Personal development: ChatGPT aids professionals in their personal growth journey by providing tailored recommendations for books, articles, and other resources.

Overall, ChatGPT stands as a valuable asset for professionals aiming to augment their expertise, skills, and overall effectiveness in their respective careers or occupations.

Using ChatGPT for Skill Enhancement

ChatGPT offers a potent avenue for professionals aiming to enhance their expertise. Here are several ways in which ChatGPT can be applied for professional growth:

1. Knowledge acquisition: Engaging with ChatGPT allows professionals to delve into various subjects, spanning from industry-specific insights to broader business fundamentals. Through interactive dialogues and inquiries, individuals can deepen their comprehension of intricate topics and remain abreast of industry trends.
2. Enhancing writing proficiency: ChatGPT serves as a resource for refining professionals' writing abilities by providing constructive feedback and suggesting improvements. Whether composing reports, proposals, or emails, ChatGPT offers guidance on grammar, style, and tone, ensuring clarity, brevity, and effectiveness in written communication.
3. Improving presentation skills: ChatGPT aids professionals in preparing

for presentations by offering guidance on content structure, organization, and delivery techniques. Professionals can rehearse their presentations with ChatGPT, receive performance feedback, and refine their approach accordingly.
4. Developing technical competencies: ChatGPT facilitates learning technical skills like coding, data analysis, and graphic design. By posing inquiries and receiving feedback, professionals can sharpen their skills and remain competitive in their respective fields.
5. Cultivating leadership capabilities: ChatGPT serves as a resource for leadership development, offering insights on effective people management, decision-making, and communication strategies. Professionals can seek advice from ChatGPT on specific scenarios or receive general guidance on enhancing leadership effectiveness.

In summary, leveraging AI-powered tools like ChatGPT can significantly contribute to professional learning and development. By harnessing its capabilities, professionals can elevate their skills, acquire fresh knowledge, and enhance their efficacy in their professional endeavors.

Individualized Educational Strategies using Artificial Intelligence

Tailoring learning plans with the aid of artificial intelligence (AI) involves leveraging AI tools to assist individuals in crafting personalized strategies for their professional growth and learning. By examining data derived from their past experiences and learning endeavors, AI can pinpoint areas of strength and weakness for professionals, subsequently proposing learning pathways that resonate with their objectives and interests. This method allows professionals to concentrate their learning endeavors on areas where they require the most enhancement, fostering skill development in a manner that is both tailored and efficient.

Utilizing ChatGPT, individuals can devise customized learning blueprints by gaining insights into the specific competencies and knowledge domains they need to cultivate. For instance, ChatGPT can scrutinize a professional's track record and offer learning suggestions based on the particular tasks they've undertaken, the tools they've utilized, and the outcomes they've attained. In doing so, ChatGPT aids professionals in leveraging their existing knowledge and experience to refine their skills in targeted ways.

Moreover, ChatGPT can recommend learning materials suited to a professional's preferred learning style and inclinations. Whether individuals favor video tutorials, interactive quizzes, written articles, or hands-on exercises, ChatGPT can analyze their learning history and preferences to propose resources that are more likely to captivate and be effective.

Ultimately, employing ChatGPT for personalized learning plans empowers professionals to optimize their developmental endeavors, fostering skill enhancement in a manner tailored to their unique requirements and preferences.

7

Work-Life Balance with ChatGPT

Utilizing ChatGPT can aid in attaining a harmonious balance between work and personal life through the automation of repetitive tasks, efficient organization of data, and timely reminders. It empowers professionals to streamline their workload, optimize time management, and alleviate stress. Leveraging AI to handle monotonous duties allows individuals to dedicate their energy to tasks of greater significance and value. Moreover, AI tools can contribute to fostering a healthier work-life equilibrium by recommending breaks, relaxation intervals, and recreational pursuits tailored to one's schedule and preferences. This proactive approach can mitigate burnout and enhance overall job contentment.

Employing AI for organizing both personal and professional aspects of life.

Harnessing AI for the management of personal and professional affairs offers significant advantages. ChatGPT, for instance, serves as a valuable tool in aiding individuals to effectively prioritize tasks and manage their time. By doing so, it empowers them to concentrate on crucial undertakings while delegating less pressing ones. Furthermore, by automating mundane tasks, individuals can free up valuable time and energy for alternative pursuits. Moreover, ChatGPT plays a pivotal role in assisting individuals in establishing both personal and professional objectives, devising strategies to attain them. This not only fosters motivation but also aids in maintaining focus. Lastly, leveraging AI tools like ChatGPT facilitates skill enhancement and knowledge enrichment through tailored learning programs. Through the integration of such AI technologies, professionals can strike a harmonious balance between their work and personal lives while making strides toward achieving their aspirations.

Using ChatGPT for Mindfulness and Stress Control

Professionals can utilize ChatGPT to handle their stress levels and engage in mindfulness practices. It can recommend mindfulness routines, lead through meditation sessions, and give advice on stress alleviation. Furthermore, ChatGPT aids in efficient workload management, empowering professionals to feel more organized and lessen feelings of being overwhelmed. It also sends prompts for breaks and motivates individuals to indulge in self-care pursuits like physical activity or quality time with family and friends. In summary, ChatGPT serves as a valuable resource for professionals seeking to prioritize their mental wellness and overall health.

8

ChatGPT for Remote Work

ChatGPT serves as an invaluable asset for remote work. With the increasing trend of companies adopting remote work setups, the demand for digital collaboration and communication tools has surged. ChatGPT can fulfill various roles:

1. Facilitating Collaboration: ChatGPT enables virtual meetings, brainstorming sessions, and project collaborations. It fosters teamwork by assisting in shared document editing, like project plans or proposals.
2. Managing Time Effectively: Remote workers can utilize ChatGPT to organize and prioritize tasks, ensuring efficient time management. It also serves as a reminder for upcoming deadlines and meetings.
3. Tailored Learning Experience: ChatGPT aids in personalized professional growth, offering recommendations for courses or reading materials based on individual interests and career aspirations.
4. Promoting Wellness and Balance: ChatGPT helps in scheduling wellness breaks and encourages employees to take necessary pauses or disconnect from work when required.
5. Virtual Support: Acting as a virtual assistant, ChatGPT addresses queries and sends reminders for essential tasks.

Overall, ChatGPT contributes to increased productivity and provides comprehensive support to remote teams, establishing itself as a valuable asset in remote work environments.

Improving Efficiency in Remote Environments

As remote work becomes increasingly common, professionals are exploring innovative methods to boost their effectiveness beyond the traditional office environment. ChatGPT emerges as a valuable resource in this endeavor, offering numerous advantages for remote workers.

One perk of utilizing ChatGPT for remote work involves streamlining repetitive tasks like scheduling and data input. By entrusting these duties to ChatGPT, professionals can economize time and concentrate on more strategic endeavors.

Furthermore, ChatGPT enhances collaboration and communication in remote work settings. It facilitates discussions, brainstorming sessions, and even virtual meetings, fostering connectivity and progress among remote teams.

Moreover, ChatGPT aids in time management, task prioritization, and information organization, enabling remote workers to efficiently manage their workload and schedules.

Lastly, ChatGPT supports personalized learning and skill development, empowering remote workers to acquire new competencies and stay abreast of industry advancements.

In summary, ChatGPT serves as an invaluable asset for remote workers seeking to optimize productivity and maintain connectivity with their colleagues.

Adjusting to working together and communicating in a virtual environment.

As remote work becomes increasingly prevalent, professionals need to adjust to new ways of collaborating and communicating. ChatGPT can significantly boost productivity in remote environments by facilitating virtual interactions and teamwork. Here are several ways in which ChatGPT can benefit professionals working remotely:

1. Virtual Meetings: ChatGPT can aid in organizing and conducting virtual meetings, enabling team members to communicate and collaborate in real-time. It can assist in creating meeting agendas, scheduling sessions, and even taking notes during discussions.
2. Collaborative Work: ChatGPT can support collaborative efforts on projects, allowing team members to collaborate on documents and other tasks simultaneously.
3. Communication: ChatGPT can facilitate seamless communication among team members, enabling swift and convenient exchange of information.
4. Time Management: ChatGPT can assist in time management, helping team members stay on top of deadlines and schedules.
5. Remote Training: ChatGPT can be utilized for remote training sessions, enabling team members to acquire new skills and enhance productivity.
6. Personalized Support: ChatGPT can offer personalized assistance to remote workers, aiding them in maintaining motivation and focus on their tasks.

In essence, ChatGPT can play a vital role in boosting productivity and fostering communication in remote work scenarios, enabling teams to collaborate effectively and efficiently regardless of their physical locations.

9

Ethical Considerations in AI-Assisted Work

When utilizing AI-driven work, it's crucial to prioritize ethical considerations to ensure responsible and equitable use of the technology. Here are some primary ethical factors that practitioners should bear in mind when employing ChatGPT or any other AI tool:

1. Clarity: Transparency regarding the utilization of AI and the data gathered is paramount. This entails offering clear insights into how AI algorithms function and their role in decision-making processes.
2. Bias Mitigation: AI tools may perpetuate bias if trained on biased data or lacking diversity considerations. Therefore, ensuring fairness and impartiality in AI algorithms is essential.
3. Privacy Protection: Given that AI tools often rely on data, including personal and sensitive information, it's imperative to handle data responsibly, adhering to relevant privacy laws and regulations.
4. Accountability: Just like any other tool, using AI demands a clear understanding of its capabilities and limitations, along with a sense of responsibility for any unintended consequences.

5. Human Oversight: AI tools should complement human decision-making rather than replace it. Professionals should exercise human judgment and oversight to ensure alignment with organizational values and objectives.

By incorporating these ethical considerations into practice, professionals can harness AI tools like ChatGPT to benefit both themselves and society as a whole.

Ensuring Ethical Utilization of AI in Workplaces

Just like any other technological advancement, the incorporation of AI in workplaces demands careful attention to ethical aspects to guarantee responsible utilization. Here are several crucial points to consider:

1. Data Privacy: AI tools rely heavily on data, which necessitates responsible and transparent data collection methods while also respecting individuals' privacy rights.
2. Bias: The efficacy of AI algorithms hinges on the quality of the data they're trained on. If this data contains biases, the algorithms will reflect them. Therefore, it's imperative to acknowledge and rectify potential biases in the data.
3. Transparency: AI algorithms often operate in opaque ways, making it challenging to comprehend the reasoning behind specific decisions. To address this, it's vital to ensure that AI decisions are transparent and explainable, facilitating understanding for individuals affected by these decisions.
4. Job Displacement: AI's capacity to automate various tasks currently performed by humans raises concerns about potential job displacement.

Hence, it's crucial to assess the impact of AI on employment and formulate policies to mitigate adverse effects.
5. Accountability: With AI increasingly making decisions with significant consequences for individuals, establishing accountability mechanisms becomes paramount. This entails setting standards for AI systems and implementing processes to challenge and rectify incorrect or unfair AI decisions.

In summary, the integration of AI into workplaces demands careful handling and consideration, ensuring that it is employed in a responsible and ethical manner.

Addressing Equity and Access Concerns

As organizations integrate AI tools and technologies, it's crucial to tackle equity and access concerns. The advantages of AI should extend to all demographics and organizations. Below are strategies for dealing with equity and access concerns in AI-supported tasks:

1. Ensure Universal Access to AI Tools: Organizations must ensure that AI tools are accessible to everyone, regardless of race, gender, age, or any other characteristic. This can be accomplished by offering training and resources to employees and ensuring that the tools are user-friendly.
2. Monitor and Correct Biases: AI tools can inherit biases from their training data. It's essential to monitor and correct any biases detected. Regularly reviewing the training data and involving diverse teams in tool development can help accomplish this.
3. Address the Digital Divide: Many individuals lack internet access or the necessary technology for AI tool usage. Organizations can bridge

this gap by providing technology and internet access to employees or partnering with community organizations to extend access to the wider community.
4. Ensure Ethical AI Use: Organizations should establish policies to ensure the ethical use of AI. This involves preventing AI from being used for discrimination, safeguarding privacy, and maintaining transparency in AI usage.
5. Incorporate Diverse Perspectives in Decision-Making: In decisions regarding AI utilization, involving individuals with diverse perspectives is crucial. This practice aids in identifying and addressing potential equity and access issues.

10

Looking Ahead: ChatGPT and the Future of Work

As AI technology progresses, it's probable that ChatGPT and similar language models will gain more significance in professional settings. AI's capacity to automate tasks, streamline processes, and offer tailored support could greatly boost productivity and performance at work. Furthermore, with the growing trend towards remote work and virtual teamwork, AI-driven tools like ChatGPT could aid in facilitating communication and collaboration among dispersed teams. Nevertheless, just like with any emerging technology, ethical considerations need to be addressed. It's crucial to ensure that AI usage in the workplace remains transparent, fair, and respects individuals' privacy. In summary, the future of work involving ChatGPT and other AI tools is poised to bring about enhanced efficiency, productivity, and collaboration.

Emerging Trends and Future Projections

Presently, AI and its impact on work environments are marked by several notable trends. These include employing natural language processing in customer service chatbots, automating repetitive tasks via robotic process automation (RPA), and leveraging machine learning for predictive analytics and data-informed decision-making. Looking ahead, AI is anticipated to continue reshaping work dynamics, ushering in advancements such as personalized learning, virtual and augmented reality integration, and the adoption of AI-driven assistants to bolster productivity and streamline operations.

As AI increasingly permeates workplaces, there's likely to be a reevaluation of valued skills and competencies. Attributes like creativity, emotional intelligence, and adaptability will gain prominence, being less susceptible to automation. Additionally, workers will need to embrace and collaborate with AI systems, necessitating the development of skills to effectively engage with and manage these technologies.

Overall, AI holds promise for enhancing workplace efficiency and productivity. However, it's imperative to approach its implementation ethically and responsibly, considering its potential impact on workers and society at large.

Getting Ready for a Work Environment Driven by AI

The growing utilization of AI within work settings is reshaping our approach to tasks, and this trajectory is anticipated to persist going forward. With the progression of AI technology, there's potential for a profound transformation across various work facets, encompassing automation, customization, and decision-making support.

Presently, several trends in AI within workplaces include:

1. Streamlining routine tasks: AI-driven automation tools are increasingly

employed for mundane, repetitive tasks like data entry and processing.
2. Tailoring work experiences: AI aids in customizing work experiences to suit individual preferences, thereby enhancing employee efficiency and effectiveness.
3. Assisting decision-making: AI's capacity to sift through vast data sets and offer insights bolsters decision-making processes.
4. Enabling remote work: AI-fueled communication and collaboration tools facilitate seamless remote work setups.

Looking ahead, AI is poised to assume an even more significant role in workplaces. Potential developments may include:

1. Heightened automation: Advancements in AI will render it capable of tackling more intricate tasks autonomously.
2. Refined personalization: AI will further refine its ability to comprehend individual requirements, leading to increasingly personalized work experiences.
3. Enhanced decision-making support: AI's proficiency in analyzing extensive data sets and furnishing actionable insights will see further improvement.
4. Deeper integration with other technologies: AI's integration with technologies like the Internet of Things and blockchain will result in more robust and efficient systems.

As AI's presence grows in the workplace, it's imperative to ensure responsible and ethical usage, addressing concerns such as bias and privacy. Organizations must deliberate on leveraging AI to enhance productivity and improve work experiences while mitigating potential adverse impacts.

www.ingramcontent.com/pod-product-compliance
Lightning Source LLC
LaVergne TN
LVHW021050100526
838202LV00082B/5417